a Pocket Bible Study & Journal

SEX

Hayley DiMarco

Hungry Planet

Revell
a division of Baker Publishing Group
Grand Rapids, Michigan

© 2008 by Hungry Planet

Published by Revell
a division of Baker Publishing Group
P.O. Box 6287, Grand Rapids, MI 49516-6287
www.revellbooks.com

Paperback edition published 2009
ISBN 978-0-8007-3412-1

Printed in the United States of America

Unless otherwise indicated, Scripture is taken from the Holy Bible, New Living Translation, copyright © 1996. Used by permission of Tyndale House Publishers, Inc., Wheaton, Illinois 60189. All rights reserved.

Scripture marked HCSB is taken from the Holman Christian Standard Bible, copyright 1999, 2000, 2002, 2003 by Holman Bible Publishers. Used by permission.

Scripture marked NKJV is taken from the New King James Version. Copyright © 1982 by Thomas Nelson, Inc. Used by permission. All rights reserved.

Scripture marked NIV is taken from the HOLY BIBLE, NEW INTERNATIONAL VERSION®. NIV®. Copyright © 1973, 1978, 1984 by International Bible Society. Used by permission of Zondervan. All rights reserved.

Creative direction: Hungry Planet
Interior design: Sarah Lowrey Brammeier

Contents

It's PB&J time. Time to feast on the hearty protein of God's Word mixed with the sweet goodness of grace. Let the truth stick to the roof of your mouth and satisfy your hunger. This study will offer a quick meal on the subject of sex. In it you can expect to learn what abstinence is, what sex is, and what your thoughts have to do with sexual sin. Unlike other Bible studies, this one will help you by giving you the answers you look for when you want to know how far is too far. It isn't just a fill-in-the-blank, hope-you-got-it-right kind of study. It's a guided tour of God's Word, filled with helpful suggestions and truths as well as thought-provoking and self-examining questions.

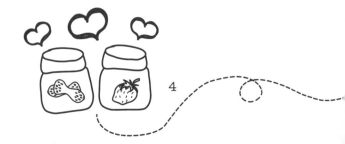

This Book

This is a study that you can do by yourself or in a group. You can lead a group of your peers or find an adult to lead it for you. Just go online at **www.hungryplanet.net** and download the leader's guide of your choice, and you are off and running!

One more note: This study is for teens and young adults, not for preteens or wannabe teens. It's for people who are ready to hear the harsh truth about sex and all the stuff that surrounds it. So it's not for the faint of heart. It's the truth in plain and simple terms—no tip-toeing around with generic or euphemistic terms. It's the straightforward truth about sex and God's plan for your sexual future.

So I hope you enjoy! Now sit down and take a bite.

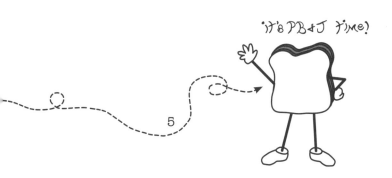

It's PB&J time!

Your Study Crew

What's up?

Okay, now just some notes to get you started. First of all let me say that I hope you are doing this book with at least one other person of the same sex. Repeat: they have to be of the same sex as you. I'm sure it would be fun to do it with your significant other, but my advice is not to do that. Studying God's Word together has a way of creating intimacy, and with that feeling of intimacy comes a greater risk of temptation. When couples who aren't yet engaged do studies together, they can become so turned on by the spirituality of it all that they lose sight of the dangers of being intimate with someone they aren't married to. And in some instances people have used the illusion of spirituality to seduce another person—using talk of spirituality for their own sexual gain. I'm not saying that your bf/gf is like that; I'm just saying, it happens. So find someone of the same sex as you to do this study with, please, please, please!

Make a list!
Who's in your crew?

It's the best way to be honest with yourself and with God while you do the study and also to guard your heart and body at the same time.

Okay, now that I've given that speech, let me just encourage you to find at least one of your buds to do this with. Sure, you can do it on your own, but with a friend or a group of same-sex friends you'll get much more out of it. It's a great way to have accountability and share God-conversations and revelations. As you work through the questions and talk about them with each other, you'll learn much more than if you just do it alone.

Once you get your gang together and they all get their books, make plans to meet once a week to go over one chapter. Be prepared to be honest and talkative. Don't just give yes and no answers; be real, dig deep, and share. That's the best way to study and to learn. The more you can learn about God's thoughts and his plans for your life as a believer, the more healthy and happy your life will become. So call a friend or two or three and get this study started!

Note for Group Leaders:

Hey, don't forget to check out the leader's guides on our website. There are two. One is for an adult leading the group and one is for you if you want to lead your friends. A guide will help you answer the hard questions and keep the gang on task. So check out www.hungryplanet.net and download that guide today!

What Is the Purpose of Sex?

This is a Bible study on sex.

That means that this book isn't for little kids or people who don't want to be exposed to any sexual talk. Like all my other books, this book is honest and pulls no punches. That means I'm gonna talk about things that other authority figures might not talk to you about. I'm going to ask hard questions and hopefully answer the things you really want to know but have been afraid to ask. Sex isn't a subject we can avoid as believers and just hope it never comes up, because if you are anywhere near anyone of the opposite sex who you are interested in, then the subject is bound to come up, at least in your mind. And the best way to be prepared with a godly response to sexual issues is to talk about them now, while you aren't under any kind of verbal or hormonal pressure. Sex can cloud your thinking and erase your memory. The promise of it can make you do out-of-character things, and without some good preparation you can end up doing something you never dreamt you would do. So if you are ready and willing, let's talk about the hush-hush subject of sex, shall we?

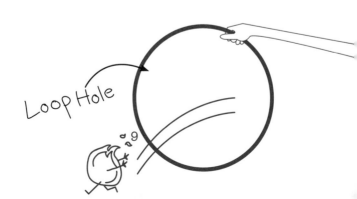

A Hot Topic

The Christian life is full of some really frustrating conflicts, but one of the biggest has to be sex. It seems so weird for God to create such an amazing thing that is oh-so-tantalizing yet so far off limits (at least in single life). For centuries—no, eons—human beings have been figuring out ways to have sex and ways to avoid having sex. It's always been a hot and a life-changing topic. Whatever your history with sex, it's definitely something that impacts your life. It's a many-faceted thing and something that you could hear lots of different things about from all kinds of different people. I can remember one particular guy presenting me with an interesting question while hoping to take my virginity when I was young. He said, "If God made sex, then he obviously wants us to enjoy it. How can it be wrong? It was God's idea." Hmmm. Interesting dilemma for a kid whose body was racing with hormones. Whatever philosophical questions you've considered on the subject or loopholes you've found to try to have all the fun without the guilt, it's time to get the facts straight from the source. But before we do that, let's talk about you:

1. What is some stuff you'd like to learn about God's take on sex?

10

Such an **amazing blessing** can also be a curse if it is used **improperly**

2. What do you think are the purposes of sex?

3. What kinds of emotional results do people who are having sex experience?

4. What kinds of physical results can happen to people who are having sex?

5. How has your life been affected by sex? Or relationships with the opposite sex?

6. Are you embarrassed to talk about sex? Why or why not?

7. Do/did your parents ever talk about sex?

8. Do you talk with your friends about sex?

those with
Questions
raise their
hands

Sex can be a super hard topic to talk about tastefully, and I'm not the most tasteful talker (yes, I'm aware). But we've got to talk about the difficult stuff, and what better place to do it than in a study of God's Word? I hope I didn't scare you off with all this personal questioning, but it was necessary to set the stage for the rest of the stuff in this book. God has some pretty direct stuff to say on the topic, so with eyes wide open and hearts ready to hear both the easy and the tough stuff, let's dig into God's Word and the subject of sex.

What Is the Purpose of Sex?

Read Genesis 2:23–24

> "'At last!' Adam exclaimed. 'She is part of my own flesh and bone! She will be called "woman," because she was taken out of a man.' This explains why a man leaves his father and mother and is joined to his wife, and the two are united into one."

1. Why do you think Adam said, "At last!"?

2. Why is Adam calling Eve part of his flesh and bone?

3. How is that different from the final phrase "the two are united into one"?

4. What does it mean for two to become one?

5. In what ways could you say that a guy and a girl who have sex have become one?

Read Genesis 1:28

> "God blessed them and told them, 'Multiply and fill the earth and subdue it. Be masters over the fish and birds and all the animals.'"

1. What three things did God command the first man and woman to do?

2. This may seem obvious, but how does one multiply and fill the earth?

Totally worth waiting for

At last!

14

3. What about this blessing and command from God is good? Are some of the duties Adam and Eve are given here potentially difficult or less desirable?

Read Proverbs 5:18–19

> "Let your wife be a fountain of blessing for you. Rejoice in the wife of your youth. She is a loving doe, a graceful deer. Let her breasts satisfy you always. May you always be captivated by her love."

1. Circle five benefits of marriage found in this description of a wife.

2. Why do you think he refers to a wife as a loving doe and a graceful deer?

3. Based on this verse, what could you guess is one of the benefits of sex?

4. What does it mean to be "captivated" by love?

15

Sex was an amazing creation by God. He had a really great idea for how to propagate the species and give the species a gift all at the same time. Do you think God would have made sex so amazing if its only purpose was to allow us to multiply? He also created it for our satisfaction and as a way for two to become one. But such an amazing blessing can also be a curse if it is used improperly, as many a broken heart can testify. Sex is something so powerful that no one can deny the hold it can have on you physically and emotionally. So I'm glad you're doing this study to find out more about why God created sex and how he wants you to handle it.

Wrapping Up

I hope this first week's study has given you some things to think about. It's only going to get more personal from here. So before you dive into the rest of the book, spend some time alone with God. Get someplace quiet and get serious. Remember, there's no hiding anything from God, so fess up your activities and your fantasies and talk to him about your desire to please him and understand his Word. Prep yourself for your time in the Bible and make some commitments to take what you learn and really apply it to your life. I'll leave you for now with a verse to help you reflect:

> But seek first his kingdom and his righteousness, and all these things will be given to you as well.
>
> Matthew 6:33 NIV

Lets Go!

What Is Abstinence?

Abstinence. Big word. Big concept.

But what does it really mean? The average bear would say that it means something like not having sex. Seems simple enough. But then, tell me why researchers have found that teens who pledge abstinence are just as likely to get STDs as teens who don't. Oops! Where's the confusion? How can you abstain from sex and still get "sexually" transmitted anythings? It's a puzzling question, but one that is easily figured out with a little Q & A. So before we dive into God's Word let's dive into your mind and talk about your thoughts on the topic of abstinence:

Abstinence—For or Against It?

1. Do you believe you have the "gift of celibacy"?

2. What is the definition of abstinence?

3. Have you signed or agreed to any kind of abstinence pledge?

Average Bears

hugs are great

19

sex can wait

sigh...

4. If so, then what does that mean to you? How far is too far for you and your pledge?

5. Do you know people who have signed pledges but are having sex?

6. Have you done things sexually that you feel guilty about?

7. Have you done things sexually that you don't feel guilty about?

8. What's the most important thing you want to learn about sex by the end of this study?

Any discussion on sex is bound to be uncomfortable. If you are really going to be honest with yourself and your crew, then there is going to be some tough stuff to talk about. Sex is an issue for all of us, so you aren't alone. And it's not the end of the world if you've messed up.

Whether you've messed up and regret it or feel fine about your choices, **it's important to know God's take on the situation.** Without a clear **understanding** of his thoughts on **everything** you do, it's hard to be **truly holy.**

What *is* important is that you want to know God and his Word and you want to get right. Whether you've messed up and regret it or feel fine about your choices, it's important to know God's take on the situation. Without a clear understanding of his thoughts on everything you do, it's hard to be truly holy. So let's take a look into God's thoughts on the topic of abstinence and sex.

What Is Abstinence?

According to *Nelson's New Illustrated Bible Dictionary*, abstinence is "the voluntary, self-imposed, and deliberate denial of certain pleasures, such as food, drink, and sex."

After looking at that definition what do you notice about abstinence? The first two adjectives should give it away. Abstinence is up to you. No one is gonna force you into it. It's a deliberate choice to deny yourself of something you like or want.

Abstinence isn't used for avoiding just sex but other things as well. A person can abstain from anything that they really want or fear will become an idol. When you abstain, you abstain from good things, not bad things. So abstinence is giving up doing what you would like to do. And that's where the usefulness of abstaining comes in. Abstinence serves a holy purpose. It teaches, purifies, and proves who you are to yourself, to others, and to God.

22

Read 1 Thessalonians 4:3–5 (NKJV)

"For this is the will of God, your sanctification: that you should abstain from sexual immorality; that each of you should know how to possess his own vessel in sanctification and honor, not in passion of lust, like the Gentiles who do not know God."

1. According to this verse, what is God's will for you?

2. What is the way of sanctification found here?

3. What does God want you to know how to do?

4. Why do you suppose God would command something like this?

Sanctification:

The process of God's grace by which the believer is separated from sin and becomes dedicated to God's righteousness (*Nelson's New Illustrated Bible Dictionary*).

Read 1 Peter 2:11–12 (NKJV)

"Beloved, I beg you as sojourners and pilgrims, abstain from fleshly lusts which war against the soul, having your conduct honorable among the Gentiles, that when they speak against you as evildoers, they may, by your good works which they observe, glorify God in the day of visitation."

1. What are you commanded to abstain from in this verse?

2. What are some fleshly lusts you can think of?

3. Why are you being asked to abstain?

Abstinence Takes Self-Control

Did you know that abstinence takes self-control? You did if you've been practicing it. And if you haven't, then look at it this way: abstinence is your chance to get really good at self-control. People who want to abstain

but mess up and do whatever it is they are abstaining from anyway say things like "I couldn't control myself." And "I just lost control." That's because abstinence is all about controlling yourself.

Self-control is such a key component of abstinence that we need to take a closer look at it in order to figure out what abstinence really is. So let's have a look.

A Word Study

According to *Merriam-Webster's Collegiate Dictionary*, to abstain is "to refrain deliberately and often with an effort of self-denial from an action or practice."

1. Why would self-denial be beneficial?

2. How could you make your practice of abstinence more deliberate?

3. Do you think that abstaining from something should take effort? What benefit does that effort give you as a believer?

Read Galatians 5:22–23

"But when the Holy Spirit controls our lives, he will produce this kind of fruit in us: love, joy, peace, patience, kindness, goodness, faithfulness, gentleness, and self-control. Here there is no conflict with the law."

1. According to this verse, where will your self-control come from?

2. If you knew that God was on your team, how confident would you be that you would win?

3. Who controls your life?

Read Proverbs 25:27

"A person without self-control is as defense-less as a city with broken-down walls."

1. What purpose did a wall serve a city in biblical days?

2. What would happen to a city with a broken-down wall?

3. What happens to you when your walls break down?

Read 2 Peter 1:5–7

"A life of moral excellence leads to knowing God better. Knowing God leads to self-control. Self-control leads to patient endurance, and patient endurance leads to godliness. Godliness leads to love for other Christians, and finally you will grow to have genuine love for everyone."

1. According to this verse, what is the start of knowing God better?

2. And what does it say is the source of self-control?

27

3. What are the three benefits of self-control?

4. In what ways could abstinence lead to godliness according to this verse?

A truly godly life requires self-control, and God has commanded you to have self-control when it comes to your sex life. Abstinence is your chance to prove your self-control and obedience to God. Though it can be really tough it can also give you tons of rewards. So remember that there is more to abstinence than just doing what you're told; it's doing the opposite of what you really, really want. That self-denial is what builds your godly character and proves yourself to God and to those around you.

Practicing Abstinence (and Self-Control)

Okay, so we've looked into abstinence and why it's a good idea for you in your life. Now how about finding out more about how to put it into action? Sometimes it can be easier said than done, and that's why so many people mess up. So let's see if we can't get some practical info about abstinence and you from God's Word.

Abstinence Take 1

A truly **godly** life requires
self-control,
and God has
commanded you to have
self-control
when it comes to your
sex life.
Abstinence is your chance
to prove your
self-control
and obedience to God.

Read 1 Corinthians 6:18–20

"Run away from sexual sin! No other sin so clearly affects the body as this one does. For sexual immorality is a sin against your own body. Or don't you know that your body is the temple of the Holy Spirit, who lives in you and was given to you by God? You do not belong to yourself, for God bought you with a high price. So you must honor God with your body."

1. What distinguishes sexual sin from other sins according to this verse?

2. What does Paul say is the purpose of your body?

3. What kinds of things dishonor God with your body?

4. Have you ever felt like you have dishonored God with your body? How did you feel afterward?

5. If you knew you were in charge of the temple of God what would you do? How would you take care of the temple where your God lived?

6. What are some ways that you can protect the temple, your body, from pollution and sin?

Read Colossians 3:5

"So put to death the sinful, earthly things lurking within you. Have nothing to do with sexual sin, impurity, lust, and shameful desires. Don't be greedy for the good things of this life, for that is idolatry."

1. Circle all the sins this verse says to put to death.

2. Which of them have to do with sexual sin?

3. In your own words what would you consider "sexual sin"?

Read Genesis 2:24

"This explains why a man leaves his father and mother and is joined to his wife, and the two are united into one. Now, although Adam and his wife were both naked, neither of them felt any shame."

1. What does "united into one" mean?

2. What must a man do before being joined to his wife?

3. Why was it okay for both Adam and Eve to be naked together?

4. According to this verse when is sex okay and not shameful or sinful?

Dude, your epidermis is showing.

32

SELFIX
CONTROLTICUS
THE ABSTAINER

Read Proverbs 5:15

"Drink water from your own well—share your love only with your wife. Why spill the water of your springs in public, having sex with just anyone? You should reserve it for yourselves. Don't share it with strangers."

1. According to this verse, when is sex permitted?

2. Who are you not to have sex with?

Read Romans 14:23

"But if people have doubts about whether they should eat something, they shouldn't eat it. They would be condemned for not acting in faith before God. If you do anything you believe is not right, you are sinning."

In Paul's day eating certain foods could be considered a sin. There were lots of people still practicing Judaism who didn't yet know what they could and couldn't do. So with that in mind answer the following questions.

1. According to this verse, what is a sin?

2. Do you think that you have been or are going too far sexually?

3. How do you feel after you've gone too far?

4. If you apply this verse to your sex life, how can it help you steer clear of sexual sin?

Beware of taking on the **world's** sense of right and wrong, because when we do **we turn our backs on our God.**

So are you getting the idea of what kind of rules God has about sex? Kind of a no-brainer. You've heard it all before, but it's important to know what's allowed and what's not. The next question you might have is, Okay, so I'm not married, but how far is too far? And that's a great question. So great that I saved an entire chapter for it. So let's finish up with this and then we'll move onto that stuff.

Know What Is Forbidden

Read Exodus 20:14

> "Do not commit adultery."

1. What is adultery?

2. Why do you think God would include adultery as one of the ten commandments?

It's so important for you to understand how valuable the marital and sexual relationship is to God. The world around us has weakened that bond. And many people no longer see fooling around as much of a sin. But we have to beware of taking on the world's sense of right and wrong, because when we do we turn our backs on our God.

Read Matthew 15:19–20 (KJV)

> "For out of the heart proceed evil thoughts, murders, adulteries, fornications, thefts, false witness, blasphemies: These are the things which defile a man: but to eat with unwashen hands defileth not a man."

1. Look at the list of evil thoughts. Are there any that seem less evil than others?

2. How do all of them "defile a man"?

3. What do you consider fornication or "sexual misconduct"?

4. What do your parents consider "sexual misconduct"? How about your pastor?

5. In the beginning of this verse Jesus call them "evil thoughts." How can thoughts alone "defile" you?

Read Romans 1:26–27

"That is why God abandoned them to their shameful desires. Even the women turned against the natural way to have sex and instead indulged in sex with each other. And the men, instead of having normal sexual relationships with women, burned with lust for each other. Men did shameful things with other men and, as a result, suffered within themselves the penalty they so richly deserved."

1. According to this verse what desires are shameful?

2. What was the result of these desires being acted upon?

Fornication:

In the New Testament, almost any form of sexual misconduct (that is, sexual activity outside the marriage relationship) could be designated as fornication or "immorality" (Harper's Bible Dictionary).

Read Deuteronomy 27:21

"Cursed is anyone who has sexual intercourse with an animal."

1. According to this verse what kind of sex is unlawful?

2. What happens to anyone who has this kind of sex?

Read Leviticus 18:6

"You must never have sexual intercourse with a close relative, for I am the Lord."

1. According to this verse what kind of sex is immoral?

2. How many guilty parties are involved if the incest was consensual? How many are guilty of sin if it was forced? Why the difference?

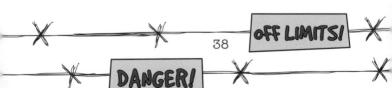

Read Leviticus 19:29

"Do not defile your daughter by making her a prostitute, or the land will be filled with promiscuity and detestable wickedness."

1. What kind of sexual sin is listed here?

2. What would be the outcome of this sexual sin?

3. Here's an interesting fact. Check out the definition of prostitution: the act or practice of indulging in promiscuous sexual relations, especially for money. What would the word *especially* insinuate in this instance?

4. Now take a look at the word *promiscuous*: not restricted to one sexual partner. With that def. in mind, rewrite the definition of prostitution.

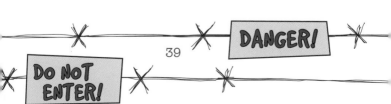

5. What kind of sexual sin could now be listed as part of Leviticus 19:29?

After reading this far have you changed your definition of sexual immorality? Are there things you've added or taken away? What makes something sexual? And what makes it bad? Are there things you've been doing that you are going to stop doing or thinking?

Sexual immorality is a murky topic for most teens. It may feel best to just ignore it and loosely define it. That way you can plead ignorance when confronted with sin. But you can't do that any more. You've been filled in; ignorance is no longer an option. Don't fear, though, there is forgiveness and grace for you if you've just been enlightened to your sin. You didn't used to know what you know now, and God gets that. Now it's a matter of what you do from here on out. What is your new definition of sex and how far will you now go?

Wrapping Up

Abstinence is a busy word. It gets thrown around all over the place, but does everyone really know what it means? And most importantly, do you? Hopefully you do now and you'll have a better time practicing it as you begin dating or keep dating. Remember that as a believer your goal should be godliness, and deciding to practice the self-control of abstinence is a step in that direction. In the next lesson, we'll dive into more of God's ideas on how far you can go before you've moved out of abstinence and into sexual sin. But first, here's a verse to cap off what we studied this week. Make it your motto for how you're going to live.

> And so, dear brothers and sisters, I plead with you to give your bodies to God. Let them be a living and holy sacrifice—the kind he will accept. When you think of what he has done for you, is this too much to ask? Don't copy the behavior and customs of this world, but let God transform you into a new person by changing the way you think.
>
> Romans 12:1–2

Week 3

How Far Is Too Far?

Sex is a big tripping point for a lot of Christians.

It's not something usually done in public, like gossiping or lying, and so it's easy to keep secret. But more importantly, it's easy to deceive yourself as well. It's not that you don't know what you are doing physically but that you aren't willing to get real with yourself about how far is too far in God's eyes. Everyone seems to draw their own line and come up with their own definition of sexual immorality. But not anymore. It's time for all of us to get real and to dig into the lies and loopholes that we all have created in some way or another when it comes to sex. Be warned: this section is graphic. I'm not willing to skirt around the issues; they have to be talked about, and what safer place than in a Bible study with your friends? It's got to be done. So let's do it.

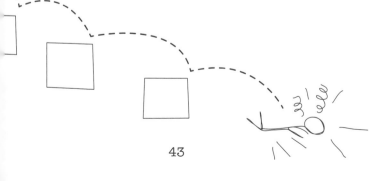

Which line?   *How far is too far?*

The Way You See It

The way you see it right now, how far is too far? Let's start with a little self-assessment—and maybe some tough confession.

1. Where do you think believers should draw the line physically?

2. Have you crossed that line?

3. Do you think that oral sex is a safe and not-so-immoral option?

4. (Circle) all the things here that you think are sinful or unbiblical for unmarried people to do:

   being skin on skin   dry humping
   oral sex   hand jobs   kissing
   sex talk   holding hands
   feeling or being felt up
   sleeping in the same bed
   heavy petting

5. Explain why the things you did not circle are not sinful in your mind.

6. Have you ever moved your line because someone convinced you that it wasn't far enough?

7. Do you think it would be good if your parents, pastor, or youth group leader would just tell you where the line is so you knew how far was too far?

8. Where do your parents draw the line when it comes to your dating life? What do you think of that?

9. Do you have friends who believe the line is somewhere other than where you think it is? Is that okay?

10. Is there one absolute line for everyone? If so, what is it?

11. Do you think it's harder for guys or girls to control themselves when it comes to sex?

12. Do you think virginity is more important to guys or girls? Why?

Okay, maybe those aren't questions you are used to reading in a Bible study, but I'm tired of Christians being afraid of the topic of sex. No talk means no understanding of truth. We've all got to stop the charade and start getting real with each other and with our God. If we don't talk about the tricky stuff, then we're more likely to just fall into the pit and not even know we've fallen. So thanks for risking embarrassment for the sake of faith. It will be worth it, I promise.

Virginity

is such an important term in

Christian culture,

but what does it

really mean?

Are You Still a Virgin?

Do you want to be a virgin till you get married? Do you think that losing your virginity before marriage is the definition of sexual immorality? Virginity is such an important term in Christian culture, but what does it really mean?

The *Merriam-Webster's Dictionary* defines virgin as "a person who has not had sexual intercourse." Makes sense, and I think we would all agree. But let me just throw one more factor into the equation. What is "sexual intercourse"? I mean, how far do you have to go in order to have had "intercourse"? Let's look up the word and see what the definition of it is:

intercourse:
physical sexual contact between individuals that involves the genitalia of *at least one person*

1. According to this definition would there have to be two naked people in order for it to be intercourse?

2. Does this mean that oral sex is considered intercourse?

According to this definition, it takes two to tango, but only one needs to be exposed. Does that change your definition of virginity at all? It may or may not, but it's something to think about when it comes to how far is too far. Do you know anyone who believes that what they have done with another person didn't really count as sex? This discussion obviously isn't about a biblical definition; it's about a dictionary definition. We are looking at the words of Merriam-Webster, but the concept has to get you thinking—at least I hope it starts the conversation about what sex really is and how far is too far.

What's Purity?

Now that you've had time to think about what sex and virginity really mean, let's talk about another popular term: purity. Purity rings, purity pledges . . . what makes a person pure?

Read the definition of **pure**

> **pure:** (1.) unmixed with any other matter; (2.) free from moral fault or guilt; (3.) chaste, i.e., innocent of unlawful sexual intercourse (*Merriam-Webster's Dictionary*).

1. Which definition do you think applies the most to sexual purity?

2. Do they all apply? How?

3. Considering these definitions, is maintaining your purity as easy as avoiding intercourse, or is there more to it? How pure is pure?

4. Think and talk about some of these situations in light of purity:

Can you sleep in the same bed, not touching each other more than kissing, and still be pure?

What about kissing in the hallway at school? Is that pure?

Can you be skin on skin with someone and still be pure?

Are you pure if you are making out with your bf or gf?

How far can you go before you are no longer pure?

Purity is such a big topic, and it means so many different things to so many different people. How do you come up with the real answer? Is there one line for everyone, or are there all kinds of lines depending on who you are? Maybe that's why sexual sin is such a big problem for so many of us—because no one really seems to have a clear answer. So how do you make your decisions? How do you know what's right and what's wrong? It's apparent from the definitions we've read that when it comes to purity, the mind is involved as well as the body. That's probably why some people feel their conscience and purity is clear before God when they kiss their crush while others have their minds racing down an impure path. Let's look at one more verse on the subject.

Read Ephesians 5:3 (NIV)

> "But among you there must not be even a hint of sexual immorality, or of any kind of impurity."

1. What are some things a couple could do that would hint about sexual stuff going on between them?

2. Is it possible to be pure and still give off hints that point to some kind of sexual immorality? How?

3. Have you ever done anything that was innocent but that someone looking on might think was sexual?

4. Why do you think God prohibits even the appearance of sexual immorality?

Not to sound like a broken record, but here goes again: how far is too far? Is your opinion changing at all? God's definition and law against sexual stuff seems a lot broader than just "don't do it!" There are other factors involved in purity, including nonsexual stuff that might *look* sexual to someone peeking in. So how do you juggle your God-given sexuality and your need for innocence and purity? Let's keep going and see if we can't find out.

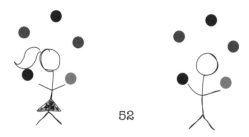

The More I Drink, the Cuter You Get!

Have you ever noticed how alcohol and sex often go together? It seems that booze has a way of making us stupid when it comes to our commitments. So let's take a look at God's take on the idea of drinking and sin.

Read Hosea 4:11

> "Alcohol and prostitution have robbed my people of their brains."

1. What does it mean to be robbed of your brain?

2. What are some of the dangers of alcohol when it comes to the topic of purity?

3. What kinds of things happen when your brain is turned off and you are with the opposite sex?

4. How might prostitution rob people of their brains?

Liquid Stupid

5. Do you think premarital sex could do the same thing?

Alcohol makes you do stupid things, and it leaves you vulnerable to stupid people. It can make you feel really brave and happy, but it can also make you do things you'd otherwise never do. If you want to be holy and obedient to God's Word, then alcohol can be a dangerous substance on your can-do list. In situations when your purity is at risk, think of it as liquid stupid.

Birds of a Feather

Birds of a feather flock together, or so the saying goes. Can you think of any people around you to whom that applies? Why do you think that saying is true? What makes people hang out with people who are like them? And how could choosing to hang out with people who really *aren't* like you be like playing with fire? When one person in a group is doing something bad, do you ever automatically assume the others are doing it as well? Who you hang out with has a lot to do with your faith—and your purity.

Alcohol makes you do **stupid things,** and it leaves you vulnerable to **stupid people.** In situations when your **purity is at risk,** think of it as **liquid stupid.**

Read 1 Corinthians 5:9–11

"When I wrote to you before, I told you not to associate with people who indulge in sexual sin. But I wasn't talking about unbelievers who indulge in sexual sin, or who are greedy or are swindlers or idol worshipers. You would have to leave this world to avoid people like that. What I meant was that you are not to associate with anyone who claims to be a Christian yet indulges in sexual sin, or is greedy, or worships idols, or is abusive, or a drunkard, or a swindler. Don't even eat with such people."

1. Who is Paul commanding the believers to avoid?

2. Why do you think God would tell you to not even eat with such people?

3. Of all the sins that could be listed here, why do you suppose these six were chosen?

4. Who is Paul telling us we *cannot* avoid?

5. What are some reasons that God would want you to be around those kinds of people?

Read 1 Corinthians 15:33

"Don't be fooled by those who say such things, for 'bad company corrupts good character.'"

1. How does this verse relate to the one we just studied?

2. How might this verse apply to someone you are dating or thinking about dating?

3. What are some of the dangers of dating (not just being friends with) a nonbeliever?

4. What are some of the dangers of dating a believer who has been sexually active?

5. What does this verse tell you about friends who might push the line farther than you?

6. Do you remember a time when a friend convinced you that something you believed was too restrictive?

7. Have you ever done the same to someone else?

The whole "birds of a feather flock together" thing isn't a cliché for nothing. As human beings we pick people to hang out with because we want to be or are like them. You have to be really careful, though, that you know who you want to be and that your friends aren't changing who you want to be without you even realizing it. Friends have a lot of control over your life, so make sure you pick the good ones.

Keep a Clear Conscience

Read 1 Timothy 1:19

"Cling tightly to your faith in Christ, and always keep your conscience clear. For some people have deliberately violated their consciences; as a result, their faith has been shipwrecked."

1. What does it mean to "keep your conscience clear"?

2. What happens if you do something that deep down you know is wrong?

3. What do feelings of guilt tell a believer about their actions?

4. Are you convinced that the line you've drawn for sex is the right line?

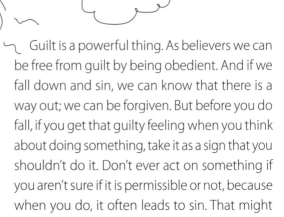

Guilt is a powerful thing. As believers we can be free from guilt by being obedient. And if we fall down and sin, we can know that there is a way out; we can be forgiven. But before you do fall, if you get that guilty feeling when you think about doing something, take it as a sign that you shouldn't do it. Don't ever act on something if you aren't sure if it is permissible or not, because when you do, it often leads to sin. That might sound harsh, but don't think of it that way. Think of it as a great way to control yourself and become more obedient to God starting today.

Wrapping Up

When it comes to deciding how far is too far, you have to be honest with yourself. Do you believe God's Word to be true? If you do, then what will you do with what you've read so far? How will it affect the line you draw when it comes to sex? Maybe you've felt guilty in the past but have pushed down that guilt and done certain things anyway. Or maybe you've just drawn the line at full-on intercourse and figured all else is free for the taking. Maybe you've done nothing wrong and are completely guilt free, and to that

I say congratulations. But whatever your history, it's important to direct your future by looking through the lens of God's Word. If you've made it this far without falling down, how will you stay the course? And if you've messed up, how will you get back on track? Deciding today how far is too far is the first place to start. You can't decide that in the heat of the moment; you have to do it now, before your hormones threaten to take over and your clothes seem just a little too anxious to come off. So how far is too far?

Talk to your study crew, your leader, your pastor, and your God and make some decisions. Don't base it on what everyone else is doing but base it on what God is doing in your heart. How much do you love him? How far will you go (or not go) to be obedient?

Week 3

> Do not let sin control the way you live; do not give in to its lustful desires. Do not let any part of your body become a tool of wickedness, to be used for sinning. Instead, give yourselves completely to God since you have been given new life. And use your whole body as a tool to do what is right for the glory of God. Sin is no longer your master, for you are no longer subject to the law, which enslaves you to sin. Instead, you are free by God's grace.
>
> Romans 6:12–14

What Are You
Thinking?

Virginity, purity, fornication, adultery, sexual immorality . . . we've covered a lot of big issues.

And hopefully you've found a few answers to your questions about sex. But if not, just hang on, because we'll get there. In this chapter we are going to look at your mind. There's more to sex than just two bodies; there's also the things that control those bodies: minds. It should come as no shock that a lot of thinking goes into both purity and sexual immorality, and it's those thoughts that are the start of it all. For now we are putting all the physical aspects of sex on the shelf, and we're going to explore your mind. What you think about and dream about and how that can be your downfall or your victory. Let's talk, shall we?

Whatcha Thinkin'?

Since this is some pretty deep interior stuff, you might not want to share it all with your crew, but I would recommend you share it with at least one close friend or trusted confidant. It's important, in the process of getting pure, to be honest about your downfalls,

your sin, because only then can you get right and move closer to your God. So give these some thought and share if you are willing, for in the end, only those who are transparent are clean. But don't go around sharing this with everyone. Make sure that the people or person you share this with won't use it against you or judge you for it. This is not an opportunity to gossip or slam each other but a chance to be open and to do something about the sin you are in.

1. How many times a day do you think about someone you are crushing on?

2. How many times a day do you think about sex?

3. Do you have any sexual or romantic fantasies you repeatedly like to daydream about?

4. Do you look at porn?

64

Oh baby
baby

5. When you see someone who is hot and turns you on, do you imagine doing sexual stuff with them?

6. Have you ever undressed someone with your eyes?

7. Do you have a favorite make out song that gets you all hot and bothered? (Luther, R. Kelly, Barry White, anyone?)

8. Have you ever gotten excited or turned on just by thinking about someone?

Week 4

9. Do you think someone is more attractive if they are a virgin or experienced? Why?

10. Have you ever exaggerated your sexual experience? Why?

By now you may be wondering, why all these questions about what you are thinking? The best way to answer that question is with a verse, so here goes.

Read James 1:14–15 (NIV)

> "Each one is tempted when, by his own evil desire, he is dragged away and enticed. Then, after desire has conceived, it gives birth to sin; and sin, when it is full-grown, gives birth to death."

1. According to this verse, what tempts you?

2. What two things does that temptation do?

3. What is then born?

4. After it's born, what happens?

5. What is the final result of this process?

Dragged away

6. It's interesting that the word *conceive* can mean several things, and they all fit this verse. Three definitions of *conceive* are (1) to take into one's mind; (2) to cause to begin; and (3) to become pregnant with. How can each of those definitions apply in this verse?

7. According to this verse, where does sin get its start?

Read Proverbs 23:7 (HCSB)

"For as he thinks within himself, so he is."

1. What do you think about the most?

2. What do you wish you thought about more?

67

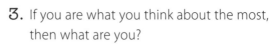

3. If you are what you think about the most, then what are you?

4. Can a person who thinks about hating be loving at the same time?

5. Can a person who thinks about sexual things all the time consider themselves to be pure?

6. How does what you think about affect your soul?

According to God's Word, thoughts have a powerful and practical impact on your life. That's why no discussion of purity would be complete without a look into your thoughts. This isn't something that a lot of people talk about, but since God hears all your thoughts, and thoughts are what lead you into sin in the first place, it makes sense that God would care a lot about what goes on in that big mind of yours, doesn't it? Let's keep looking more specifically at some do's and don'ts of your thought life.

If **sin** were measured by

keeping track of things you

think about

or look at

and not only things

you do or say,

then would you be

innocent?

Sexy Thoughts

If sin were measured by keeping track of things you think about or look at and not only things you do or say, then would you be innocent? Would you be guilty of sexual immorality? Tough question. But Jesus says it's *the* question when it comes to sex. Check it out.

Read Matthew 5:27–30

> "You have heard that the law of Moses says, 'Do not commit adultery.' But I say, anyone who even looks at a woman with lust in his eye has already committed adultery with her in his heart. So if your eye—even if it is your good eye—causes you to lust, gouge it out and throw it away. It is better for you to lose one part of your body than for your whole body to be thrown into hell. And if your hand—even if it is your stronger hand—causes you to sin, cut it off and throw it away. It is better for you to lose one part of your body than for your whole body to be thrown into hell."

God's Law

beard

Definition time! *Lust* is defined as "sinful longing" (*Easton's Bible Dictionary*) or "to have an intense desire or need" (*Webster's Dictionary*).

Mt Sinai

1. Can you relate? Is there anyone you lust over? You don't have to mention names, but be honest!

2. How can you commit a sin just by thinking about someone?

3. What is the spiritual crime here, according to Jesus?

4. What does Jesus say is the alternative to doing all you can to stop that crime?

5. Have you ever indulged in a fantasy over someone you thought was hot?

6. Have you ever lusted for someone you were "just fooling around with"?

7. How far can you go sexually without lusting?

8. What is the punishment for lust, according to Jesus?

9. According to this verse, how far is too far when it comes to your sex life?

10. Make a list of things that a guy and girl could do together that potentially could cause one of them to lust (for example, hot tubbing, napping together, back rubs). If you aren't sure how to answer this, then ask your parent of the opposite sex if the things you are thinking of would potentially turn on someone who liked you: "Dad, do you think that letting a guy see my stomach could turn him on?"

1. _____
2. _____
3. _____
4. _____
5. _____

Read Exodus 20:17

"Do not covet your neighbor's house. Do not covet your neighbor's wife, male or female servant, ox or donkey, or anything else your neighbor owns."

1. What's the topic of this verse?

2. What is the definition of *covet*? Look it up—it really helps to get a good def.

3. According to the definition, in order for you to covet something, does it have to belong to someone else?

4. What things are included in this "do not covet" list?

5. Do you covet anything sexual in your relationship or your crush?

6. What are your weaknesses when it comes to coveting other people?

Dig Deeper:

Covetousness. It's a topic I could talk about for a really long time. It's so huge and it's so normal in our daily lives. We wish for newer cars, better cells, nicer clothes; we covet hundreds of times a day. If you want to learn more about your coveting habits, dig in and do a little research. The *New Bible Dictionary* says this about covetousness: "The Hebrews visualized the soul as full of vigorous desires which urged it to extend its influence over other persons and things. . . . It is in essence the worship of self." Ouch! Beware what you "wish" you had. The Bible calls covetousness idolatry. To dig deeper, research both words in any Bible dictionary, concordance, or commentary that you can get your hands on. It's a really intense study.

Read Mark 7:21–22

"For from within, out of a person's heart, come evil thoughts, sexual immorality, theft, murder, adultery, greed, wickedness, deceit, eagerness for lustful pleasure, envy, slander, pride, and foolishness. All these vile things come from within; they are what defile you and make you unacceptable to God."

1. What do you think could be another word for your "heart" as used in this verse?

2. According to Mark, where does sexual immorality come from?

3. What does this say about your thoughts?

Read Romans 8:6–7 (NIV)

"The mind of sinful man is death, but the mind controlled by the Spirit is life and peace; the sinful mind is hostile to God. It does not submit to God's law, nor can it do so."

Before we hit the questions, take a look at *Merriam-Webster's* definition of *mind*: "the element or complex of elements in an individual that feels, perceives, thinks, wills, and especially reasons."

"I ♥ YOU."

"You heart me." "My heart is broken." "My heart hurts." "I just know it in my heart." We use the word **heart** to convey so many things. And sometimes its meaning gets kind of muddy. It can be hard to really put into words what your heart is, besides the organ that pumps blood. There's so much more to it than that. So for additional study, do some research on the heart. Check out some Bible software or online Bible dictionaries and commentaries. It's a trip how important the heart is in the mind and soul of a human being. According to *Harper's Bible Dictionary*, "The heart's function as the source of thought and reflection highlights its intellectual capacities (Isa. 6:10; Mark 7:21-23). The heart understands (Deut. 8:5; Isa. 42:25), provides wisdom to rule justly and wisely (1 Kings 3:12; 10:24), and discerns good and evil (1 Kings 2:44)." There's more to a heart than just love and kisses. So check it out!

1. Let's paraphrase the verse by replacing the word *mind* with the list from the definition of mind. I'll start you off; you fill in the remaining three blanks:

"The <u>feelings</u>, <u>perceptions</u>, _____, _____, and _____ of the sinful man are death."

2. According to Paul in these verses, what are the benefits of having your mind set on godly things? (Hint: there are two.)

3. Why do you think Paul said "the mind" instead of just saying "the sinful man is . . ."?

Week 4

4. What are some ways that a mind can be death?

5. According to this verse, how do you get life and peace instead of death?

77

It all starts here

God makes it very clear that your thoughts are what count in the grand scheme of things. He demands more of us than just good actions; he demands good thoughts. Tough demand, I know. And if you aren't used to thinking good thoughts, it's super tough to change, but it's got to be done. Your thoughts speak directly to God. All you think about, he hears. But it's not too late to change, and it's not too late to get right with God. Confess your stupid thoughts and promise never to think them again. It's time for a return to the God you love. It's time to show him in your thoughts that you love him and trust him! Think about the kinds of things on your mind most of the day. Do a thought inventory and clean house. All the bad stuff out and only good stuff in. Make a list of the things you often think about that are sinful. They could be hate, envy, lust, revenge, bitterness, lying, cheating, fooling around. Think about it. Give this some time and be honest. It's the only way to true purity. You have to start where the sin starts! So do it now.

Your Eyes and Ears

I hope you've done your thought inventory. I hope you've taken a good look at what you think about most. If you haven't, then don't go any further till you do. I'll wait for ya.

Okay, now that's done, let's focus on your eyes and ears. Thoughts can come from all kinds of places, but two of the most obvious are from your eyes and your ears. The things you look at and listen to have a major impact on what you think. In fact, sometimes those things are *all* that determine what you think. And when it comes to sex, the things you look at and listen to can make or break you in an instant.

So what do you look at or listen to? What do you allow inside your mind? Let's compare that to God's Word and see what it has to say about the objects of your senses.

Porn in the Bible

Check out one of the earliest accounts of porn addiction, found in Ezekiel 23:14–17: "Then she carried her prostitution even further. She fell in love with pictures that were painted on a wall—pictures of Babylonian military officers, outfitted in striking red uniforms. Handsome belts encircled their waists, and flowing turbans crowned their heads. They were dressed like chariot officers from the land of Babylonia. When she saw these paintings, she longed to give herself to them, so she sent messengers to Babylonia to invite them to come to her. So they came and committed adultery with her, defiling her in the bed of love. After being defiled, however, she rejected them in disgust."

Read Job 31:1

"I made a covenant with my eyes not to look with lust upon a young woman."

1. What is another word for "covenant"?

2. What did Job make a covenant with?

3. Why would Job need to make that kind of covenant?

4. What are some ways that your eyes cause you to lust?

5. What usually comes first, the looking or the lusting?

6. What are some things that might help you avoid looking in lust?

Read 1 John 2:16 (NIV)

"For everything in the world—the cravings of sinful man, the lust of his eyes and the boasting of what he has and does—comes not from the Father but from the world."

1. Why is lust linked to the eyes?

2. What do "the cravings of sinful man" and "the lust of his eyes" have in common?

3. According to this verse, where do they come from?

4. Does that make them holy or unholy?

5. Can you think of some ways that cravings and lust get to you from the world?

Week 4

Read Job 31:11–12

"For lust is a shameful sin, a crime that should be punished. It is a devastating fire that destroys to hell. It would wipe out everything I own."

1. How can Job call lust a crime if no one gets hurt?

2. How do you think that lust, or looking or listening to something that causes it, could be a "devastating fire"?

What you put into your head determines what thoughts you think. Sex isn't just about two bodies; it's about one—you. What do you see or hear that makes you lust? Certain songs, pictures, and hot bodies can be a total snare to your spiritual life. Beware of what you let your mind focus on.

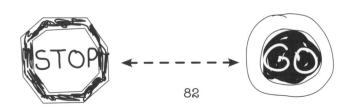

Your Secret Life

The thing about your mind is that it's a great place to hide. People can see your actions, they can hear your words, but they have no idea what's going on in your mind. What kinds of things do you hide from others? Don't let your mind be a sin pit, because you aren't the only one who knows your thoughts.

Read Ecclesiastes 12:14

> "God will judge us for everything we do, including every secret thing, whether good or bad."

1. How much of what you do will be judged?

2. Does this include what you let yourself look at and listen to?

3. Is it sinful to do something bad that doesn't affect anybody but you? Explain.

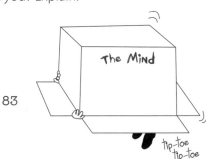

The Mind

tip-toe
tip-toe

Read Romans 2:16

"The day will surely come when God, by Jesus Christ, will judge everyone's secret life. This is my message."

1. What is the difference between your everyday, walking around life and the secret life Paul is talking about?

2. Why do you think Paul specifically mentions "everyone's secret life"?

3. What does it say will happen in the end when Jesus looks at what you did in secret?

4. Do you feel safer when you do something wrong in secret?

You might feel safe when you do things in secret. "I'm not hurting anyone," you reason. But just remember, we never do anything in secret when it comes to God. He's in on every thought and every deed. So next time you "secretly" think or do something, remember that you are not alone.

Wrapping Up

Maybe you've found out something about yourself in this chapter. Maybe you've realized that you've been thinking or doing something that isn't holy and you want to change. Well, good for you! Sex starts in your mind, so it's important to reflect on what kinds of things you are letting in. As we keep going on this track, watch your thoughts closely, and don't let anything get in that leads you to lust for what is or isn't yours. I'll leave you with a good verse to remember and maybe even memorize:

> Run from anything that stimulates youthful lust. Follow anything that makes you want to do right. Pursue faith and love and peace, and enjoy the companionship of those who call on the Lord with pure hearts.
>
> 2 Timothy 2:22

Week 5

What Are They Thinking?

So how did it feel to search your deepest, darkest, hottest thoughts?

Did what you learned shock you? I hope that it at least got you thinking about thinking. Being faithful is much more than just *doing* good. There's so much more going on below the surface that God takes just as seriously as what shows. And sexual immorality is more than just the act of intercourse. It's much, much more, and so now let's take a look at what else might lead down the path of danger that on the surface might not seem so bad.

The last chapter was all about you—your mind, your fantasies, your secrets. But this chapter is all about *them*. The opposite sex. What they are thinking and dreaming about and how you influence that, and thus how responsible you are for that.

Here's Looking at You

Let's start with the usual Q&A:

1. On a scale of 1 to 10, how hot would you say others say you are?

2. Have you ever used your body to get the attention of the opposite sex?

3. What's your best physical feature?

4. What is a tease?

5. If a guy gets led on by a girl who doesn't really like him, whose fault is it?

6. What does it take to turn a guy on?

7. What kinds of things usually get girls turned on by or interested in guys?

8. List five things that you love about the opposite sex.

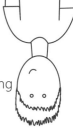

9. How far is too far when it comes to dressing hot?

10. What does God say about tempting others?

11. Have you ever been called a tease?

This chapter is all about taking a look at yourself through the other person's eyes. That means you're going to have to get over a few preconceived notions and be willing to admit that the opposite sex isn't crazy or weird when it comes to how they think . . . they are just opposite! They are called that for a reason—because it's true. Guys and girls are turned on by totally different things most of the time. And because of that, it's sometimes hard to think about how you might affect others sexually and spiritually. So let's see if we can't help you look at things from the other side of the fence.

Opposites Attract

It should come as no surprise that guys and girls are different. Very few would argue with me on that.

It's a girl thing.

But it seems like when we start talking about those differences from a dating perspective, some people get ticked off. They don't like the fact that guys and girls are different, and they want complete sameness. They might use a word like *equality*, but usually they are arguing for sameness 'cept for the plumbing. But that takes all the fun out of it. Who wants to date someone who's exactly the same as themselves? It's our differences that attract us to each other. And I don't mean different religions or different cultures; I mean feminine attracts masculine and vice versa. Differences are amazing and should be owned proudly.

Clichés are clichés for a reason. We get used to one group of people being a certain way, and so we create a cliché or a stereotype. And that is true for guys and girls and how they typically think and act. There are some generalized differences that have become clichés because they are usually true. So let's check out some of those differences.

1. In the list below, circle all the things that you think describe girls more than guys, in general, and leave the things describing guys uncircled.

   strong soft gentle tough active
   thoughtful sweet heroic aggressive
   physical emotional talkative nurturing
   valiant

2. Talk about some accepted clichés or generalizations about your gender that bug you.

3. What are some generalizations about the opposite sex that you totally agree with?

4. What is a feminine adjective you could use to describe a guy that might tick him off?

5. What is a way that you could describe a girl in a masculine way that would hurt her feelings?

6. Why do you think we are affected by being described in terms not generally used to describe our own sex?

Okay, now let's just take a really quick look at a couple of verses that might tell us something about differences between the genders.

Week 5

Read 1 Peter 3:7

"In the same way, you husbands must give honor to your wives. Treat her with understanding as you live together. She may be weaker than you are, but she is your equal partner in God's gift of new life. If you don't treat her as you should, your prayers will not be heard."

1. What distinction does this verse make between guys and girls?

2. In what ways are girls "weaker" than guys?

3. In what ways are they stronger?

4. What is the result for men who do not treat their wives right?

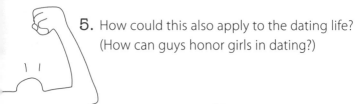

5. How could this also apply to the dating life? (How can guys honor girls in dating?)

Read 1 Peter 3:3–5

"Don't be concerned about the outward beauty that depends on fancy hairstyles, expensive jewelry, or beautiful clothes. You should be known for the beauty that comes from within, the unfading beauty of a gentle and quiet spirit, which is so precious to God. That is the way the holy women of old made themselves beautiful."

1. In the verse above, (circle) all the things Peter tells girls *not* to be concerned about.

2. Which one word that you circled best describes the theme of this verse?

3. What things on this list do you think are still an obsession for girls?

4. Girls, what things on this list are your biggest obsessions, if any?

93

5. How could those things lead to spiritual trouble?

6. Why do you think this verse is directed at girls and not at guys?

7. How might this verse confirm the differences between guys and girls?

Read Deuteronomy 22:5

"A woman must not wear men's clothing, and a man must not wear women's clothing. The Lord your God detests people who do this."

1. What could clothing have to do with godliness?

2. Why do you think God is so "detesty" about this topic?

Does this outfit make me look holy?

3. How might this apply to girls acting like guys and vice versa?

As you can see, in a brief study of God's Word we can easily find differences between guys and girls, or at least get the feeling that God made us different and wants it kept that way. So what does all this talk have to do with sex? Good question. Let's take a look, shall we?

Sex and the Opposite Sex

The truth is that guys and girls are usually turned on by different things, and that's important to understand because what you do can affect the spiritual lives of those around you without you even knowing it. If you don't know what turns people on, then you might be making the people around you crazy. And that's wrong why? Spiritual responsibility! Believe it or not, you are in some way responsible for the sexual sins of those around you, even if you aren't thinking about them or doing anything with them. Make sense? Probably not yet. Read on, my friend.

Wassup?

Guys Are Turned On by What They See

Don't need the Bible to prove this to be true. I think we all get it. Why else would porn be so popular with guys and not as much with girls (unless we're talking about paintings of Babylonian soldiers)? Guys are turned on by the sight of girly flesh, at least most guys. So what does that tell girls about their responsibilities?

1. Girls who dress sexy are responsible for guys who get turned on by them. □ True □ False

2. Guys should be able to control themselves and look away. □ True □ False

3. Girls should be concerned about guys' weaknesses. □ True □ False

4. Guys might fall into less sexual temptation if girls dressed less sexy. □ True □ False

For an extra-interesting way to discuss these, answer them yourself and then ask three people of the opposite sex the same questions. Don't say a word in response; just mark their answers so you can talk about them with your crew. It should make for some good conversation.

Romantic music

Girls Are Turned On by Romance

Dancing

Historically girls haven't been turned on by the masculine form. I mean, it can be fun to ogle, but romance addiction is much more prevalent with girls than porn addiction is. Take for example chick flicks. Girls love 'em! Why? Not because of all the beefcake but because of the romance, the gifts, the sweet talk. Mmmmm . . . girls love it. And most dream of the stuff chick flicks are made of. So what might that tell guys about their responsibility in leading girls to stumble sexually?

1. Guys who use lines or sweet talk to get girls are just being mean. ☐ True ☐ False

flowers

2. Girls might go farther sexually than they want to if a guy is saying "But I love you."
☐ True ☐ False

3. Guys shouldn't say one thing and mean another. ☐ True ☐ False

4. Girls can easily fall for a super romantic guy, even if he's not super hot. ☐ True ☐ False

Do the same thing here after you answer these yourself: If you are a guy, ask three girls or women these same questions and see what kind of response you get. And girls, ask three guys their opinions. Then talk about the answers with your study crew.

Week 5

Candle lit dinners

What you do

can **affect** the

spiritual lives

of those around you

without you even

knowing it.

Spiritual Responsibility

Here's a story problem for you: If you have a friend who is a recovering alcoholic and he's been sober five months and doing well, do you take a case of beer over to his house to drink while you watch the game? Or do you feel some kind of spiritual responsibility when it comes to his weakness? Of course to answer that, you have to answer the bigger question: What is spiritual responsibility? Spend a few minutes sharing your ideas on that. Once you've done that, let's get into some verses.

Read 1 Corinthians 8:9

> **"But you must be careful with this freedom of yours. Do not cause a brother or sister with a weaker conscience to stumble."**

1. What do you think "to stumble" means?

2. How can the female body cause a guy to stumble?

3. How could sweet talk and romance cause a girl to stumble?

4. If guys are turned on by what they see (and they are!), then how could a girl turn a guy on without even realizing it?

5. Why should you be careful with your freedom when it comes to your sexuality?

6. What are some ways that the freedom to be hot could be a sin?

7. Girls, how responsible do you feel for leading guys to stumble by how you dress?

8. Guys, how responsible do you feel for leading girls to stumble by what you say or do?

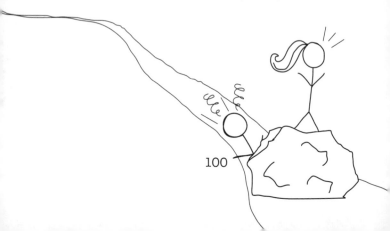

Read Romans 14:13

"So don't condemn each other anymore. Decide instead to live in such a way that you will not put an obstacle in another Christian's path."

1. What does this verse say to people who think the opposite sex just needs to learn to control themselves and get over things?

2. What kinds of "obstacles" that could cause the opposite sex to fall could you put in the way when it comes to sexuality? Make a list with your crew.

Guys	Girls

Read 1 Corinthians 10:23–24

"You say, 'I am allowed to do anything'—but not everything is helpful. You say, 'I am allowed to do anything'—but not everything is beneficial. Don't think only of your own good. Think of other Christians and what is best for them."

1. What kinds of things are you allowed to do that might not be "beneficial" to the opposite sex?

2. We are told to be concerned for what is best for others. When it comes to sexual temptation and sin, what would be "best" for the opposite sex?

Tempt:

(1.) to entice to do wrong by promise of pleasure or gain; (2.) to induce to do something (*Merriam-Webster's Collegiate Dictionary*)

Millstone

Read Matthew 18:6–7

"But if anyone causes one of these little ones who trusts in me to lose faith, it would be better for that person to be thrown into the sea with a large millstone tied around the neck. How terrible it will be for anyone who causes others to sin. Temptation to do wrong is inevitable, but how terrible it will be for the person who does the tempting."

1. How do you think that sexual activity before marriage could be an example of "losing faith"?

2. What does Jesus say to the person who tempts someone else?

3. One definition of *tempt* is "to entice to do wrong by promise of pleasure or gain." What are some things girls could do or say that might "promise pleasure or gain"?

The Modest Mermaid

4. What are some things that guys could do or say that might "promise pleasure or gain"?

5. Another definition is "to induce to do something." How could someone "induce" another to do something sexually?

6. When it comes to your actions and words, how careful do you think you need to be in the future?

Wow, what a huge responsibility you have when it comes to not only your own thoughts but also the thoughts of others. How does that make you feel? Pretty huge responsibility. More than likely you can't keep every single person around you from sinning sexually just by looking at you or listening to you, but you are being called to do your best to make sure that never happens.

Wrapping Up

A follower of Jesus is less concerned with himself than with those around him. And that's why your goal should be to care about the sexual temptation of the opposite sex. That means those you see in class, in the hall, at the mall, at church, at home, everywhere. You have to start thinking not only about yourself but also about others. It seems like a huge task for some, but those huge tasks are what test you, prove your obedience to God, and in the end bring your reward in the heavenlies. Trust God when it comes to what you think and what you do, and in the end your life will be better for it, I promise!

> Do nothing out of selfish ambition or vain conceit, but in humility consider others better than yourselves. Each of you should look not only to your own interests, but also to the interests of others.
>
> Philippians 2:3–4 NIV

Week 5

How Do You Have

Good Sex?

Welcome to the last week of the study. Congratulations on making it this far.

We've covered some tough stuff, and I bet you've had your paradigms shifted. I hope that you've gotten some good insight out of this study and a better understanding of God's take on sex. I know how hard it is to control yourself when Mr. or Miss Perfect is standing right in front of you, but the good news is that one day you won't have to. One day you can have it all—all the sex you want and with no guilt. Coolio! But before you move on from where you are, let's talk a bit about cleaning house. Let's talk about your past and how to clean up to prepare for a better future. Your future hubby or wife will be all yours, and because of that the sex will no longer be off-limits, but getting rid of those messed-up memories and mistakes will only make things better. So in this last study, we're going to talk a bit about the scrubbing bubbles of grace.

Cleaning up your Past

Before we get to the goods on grace, let's do one more quick self-assessment, just to get you thinking.

1. How do you feel about your past?

2. Are there things you are going to change about how you relate to the opposite sex?

3. Are you experiencing any guilt?

4. Is there anyone you need to apologize to?

5. Is there anything you feel the need to confess?

6. If someone wanted your advice on whether or not they should sleep with someone, what would you say?

7. Have you done anything that you think is unforgivable?

8. Are you hiding from God because you don't think he can forgive you?

9. What words would you like to hear from God about your past?

10. Is there someone you are holding a grudge against because of something sexual you did with them?

11. How positive do you feel about sticking to your new thoughts on sexuality and abstinence?

12. Do you feel like you have the strength to be good?

hiding

That wasn't so hard, was it? If you have a sordid past, I hope that you can dig through it and allow God's Word to shine on it. And if you have a not-so-bad past, I hope that you will use this last chapter to learn more about the grace and forgiveness of God for other parts of your life. Two verses that always make me feel better when I think about my mess-ups are Romans 3, verses 10 and 23: "There is no one righteous, not even one.... For all have sinned and fall short of the glory of God" (NIV). Phew! What a relief to know that I'm not a freak but just like every other human being on the planet. So with that in mind, let's take a closer look at the subject of forgiveness and grace.

Confession

It's not a cliché for nothing: the first step in solving your problem or sin is admitting that you have one. And in biblical terms, that's called confession. Confession is agreeing with God that what you did was wrong and telling him and another person about it. But just how important is confession, and how do you do it right?

Read 1 John 1:9–10

"But if we confess our sins to him, he is faithful and just to forgive us and to cleanse us

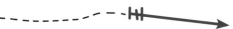

from every wrong. If we claim we have not sinned, we are calling God a liar and showing that his word has no place in our hearts."

1. According to this verse, what does confession come before?

2. Do you think that you can be forgiven without confessing?

3. So how important is confessing?

4. What is the opposite of confessing, according to the second sentence of this verse?

5. Why would that be calling God a liar?

6. Do you believe God ever lies? If so, what things has he lied to you about?

Read Proverbs 28:13

"People who cover over their sins will not prosper. But if they confess and forsake them, they will receive mercy."

1. What happens when you try to cover up your sin?

2. What two things are required in order to receive mercy?

A Liar Note:

If you believe God is a liar, then check what you think he has lied about with his Word, the Bible. Perhaps he didn't lie but didn't truly say what you thought he said. The only way to know for sure what God is saying is to read his Word. So before you call him a liar, check the facts to make sure you weren't buying a lie from someone else.

Pants on Fire

3. What does the word *forsake* mean to you?

4. Have you ever forsaken anything or anyone? If so, why?

Read James 5:16

"Confess your sins to each other and pray for each other so that you may be healed. The earnest prayer of a righteous person has great power and wonderful results."

1. According to James, what is the benefit of confessing your sins to other people?

2. Do you know any safe people you could confess things to?

3. How do you feel when you confess something stupid to someone?

4. How might that stop you from doing the stupid thing again in the future?

5. Is this verse a command or a suggestion?

6. Why do you think God wants you to tell others your junk?

Confession is the first step in calling a duck a duck and agreeing with God that he's right and you're wrong. Without a verbal agreement that sin is sin, you won't begin to heal. And without a verbal assent that Jesus is the Lord of your life, you won't be saved. God is very big on talking. He wants us to be honest and to confess when we mess up. It's healing and it's righteous. And knowing that you'll have to confess that thing you are about to do can also be a good reason to *not* do it. So give confession a try. Do it right now. Make a list, either right here or in your head, of the stupid things you've done sexually. Tell God he was right and you were wrong. Agree with him and thank him for his forgiveness and the healing that he promises. Do that and you are on your way to a better life a much better life!

Duck

Confessing to Another Person

Dear God, I confess that I . . .

Before you get too far in your confession to another person, let me just give this disclaimer: don't confess to someone who will be hurt by what you say or who you can't trust with what you say. Confession is just a chance for you to be honest with another human being about your sin and for them to offer you the truth about God and his grace and forgiveness. So don't confess to a nonbeliever, and don't confess to a gossip. If you've had lustful thoughts about someone (and they have no idea), don't confess it to them and risk hurting them or, even worse, tempting them with your shared thoughts! So find that one person you can trust who will love you anyway and who will offer you grace.

Grace and Forgiveness

They say that grace is an amazing thing, but that is easy to forget when you're feeling bad about all you've done wrong. But it can't be forgotten because it has everything to do with God's forgiveness. So for now, let me be the person who brings you the sweet taste of the grace of God that heals your wounds and sets you free from bondage.

Read Romans 3:24–25

> "Yet now God in his gracious kindness declares us not guilty. He has done this through Christ Jesus, who has freed us by taking away our sins. For God sent Jesus to take the punishment for our sins and to satisfy God's anger against us."

1. After reading this verse, do you believe that forgiveness is something you have to beg for or work for?

2. According to this verse, what happened to the punishment for your sin? Why didn't you get it?

3. Is there a sin in your past that you believe God can't forgive? Why?

4. After you confess your sins, how long do you think it is before you are set you free?

Read Ephesians 2:1–5, 8–9 (NIV)

"As for you, you were dead in your transgressions and sins, in which you used to live when you followed the ways of this world and of the ruler of the kingdom of the air, the spirit who is now at work in those who are disobedient. All of us also lived among them at one time, gratifying the cravings of our sinful nature and following its desires and thoughts. Like the rest, we were by nature objects of wrath. But because of his great love for us, God, who is rich in mercy, made us alive with Christ even when we were dead in transgressions— it is by grace you have been saved. . . . For it is by grace you have been saved, through faith—and this not from yourselves, it is the gift of God—not by works, so that no one can boast."

1. What do you think it means to be "dead in your transgressions and sins"?

2. Who is "the ruler of the kingdom of the air"?

3. What relationship do those who are disobedient have with God?

4. What is the opposite of being "dead in transgression"?

5. According to the last sentence, what saved you?

Grace defined

Grace is when someone, especially someone in authority, shows partiality or kindness to someone who doesn't deserve it. One of the most important things to know about God is that he is gracious. The Lord God is "merciful and gracious, longsuffering, and abounding in goodness and truth" (Exodus 34:6 NKJV). What's the difference between grace and mercy? Think of it like this: grace is getting something you don't deserve, and mercy is not getting what you do deserve.

6. What does grace have to do with "works"?

7. How do you get grace?

Read Psalm 103:12

> "He has removed our rebellious acts as far away from us as the east is from the west."

1. What does God do with your sin when you confess it?

2. What should that mean to you?

3. Do you keep thinking about your sins (i.e., feeling guilty or worrying) even after you confess them?

4. If you do, what does that say about your faith in God's choice to remove the act far away? Do you think he is crazy, lying, or something else?

5. Can you trust God to remove your sin? How does that make you feel?

repent:

(1.) to turn from sin and dedicate oneself to the amendment of one's life;
(2.) to feel regret or contrition;
(3.) to change one's mind
(*Merriam-Webster's Collegiate Dictionary*)

If you've messed up, then thank God for grace. Don't miss this chance to accept it and get on with your life. You can start clean whenever you are ready, no matter what you've done. That applies to your sex life and all the rest of your life as well. Are you ready to take the grace and run (to God)? Then tell him so right now.

Repentance

Anytime you sin and disobey God, you must go through the same process. You confess and agree that what you did was bad, then you thank him for his grace and his forgiveness. And after that you repent. That is, you do a 180 and turn around and walk away. Walk away from the bad. Walk away from the junk. Promise never to do it again. Easier said then done, I know, especially with addictive sins like sex. But it must be done. Repentance is commanded by Jesus himself.

Read Matthew 4:17

> "From then on Jesus began to preach, 'Repent of your sins and turn to God, because the Kingdom of Heaven is near.'"

1. What is Jesus commanding that we do?

2. What are some ways you can turn away from sexual sin?

3. If you are turned away from something or someone, are you looking at it anymore? How does this practically apply to the question of how far is too far?

Read 2 Corinthians 7:10

"For God can use sorrow in our lives to help us turn away from sin and seek salvation. We will never regret that kind of sorrow. But sorrow without repentance is the kind that results in death."

1. Do you have any sorrow in your life because of some sin?

2. What is the purpose of that sorrow?

3. What happens, according to this verse, if you feel bad but don't make a change?

Repentance is an essential step in a clean start. If you want to be holy, to be obedient, and to be clean, then you've got to make some changes. Are you ready?

Think about the people in your life who will be affected by this change, this turning away. What will they think? What will you tell them? How will you deal with those who aren't turning the same direction as you? You've got to know what you'll do before you get into the situation.

Repentance

is an **essential step**

in a clean start.

If you want to be **holy,**

to be **obedient,**

and to be **clean,**

then you've got to make

some changes.

So make a plan, get good advice, and know how to deal when you are changing and the world around you isn't.

Good Sex

God isn't all "no, no, no" when it comes to sex. He wants you to enjoy it. But he wants you to do it in the right way. Of course you know the answer: marriage. He wants you to be married. For richer or for poorer, in sickness and in health, together forever. That's the kind of stuff that makes for good, safe sex. No one has to wonder if the other person loves them or is just using them. No babies have to come into the world without a daddy. It's just the best way in the world to have sex. So let's end all this sex talk on an up note.

God isn't all **"no, no, no"** when it comes to sex. **He wants you to enjoy it.** But he wants you to do it in the **right way: marriage.**

Read Ecclesiastes 9:9

"Live happily with the woman you love through all the meaningless days of life that God has given you in this world. The wife God gives you is your reward for all your earthly toil."

1. What does this verse say about a wife?

2. What are some of the rewards of marriage?

Read 1 Corinthians 7:3–5

"The husband should not deprive his wife of sexual intimacy, which is her right as a married woman, nor should the wife deprive her husband. The wife gives authority over her body to her husband, and the husband also gives authority over his body to his wife. So do not deprive each other of sexual relations."

1. What is one of the rights of being married?

2. After reading this verse, how important do you think sex in marriage is to God?

...ated thing, but when you understand ...d your sex life and you trust his Word, ...unity for a great sex life. Sex isn't ...ned of or fearful of; it's something ...was meant for. Just slow down and wait ...the time is right. God's got a perfect plan, so don't try to outdo him—you'll only fall down and get hurt.

Wrapping Up

I hope you've learned what you wanted to learn about sex. And I hope your life is now changed. If you liked this study, then don't let it stop here. Spread the word. Find another group to take through the study. Share it with youth pastors and friends. Make sure everyone out there has a chance to get right with God and learn the truth about sex. Let me leave you with a final verse which is truly my prayer for you:

> Now may the God of peace make you holy in every way, and may your whole spirit and soul and body be kept blameless until that day when our Lord Jesus Christ comes again. God, who calls you, is faithful; he will do this.
>
> 1 Thessalonians 5:23–24

ing a group
e PB&J series?

esources to get your crew

- **iFuse.com**: sign your group up in the new online social community from Hungry Planet!

- **HungryPlanet.tv**: download videos of Hayley introducing each section of the PB&J series

- **HungryPlanet.net**: download free leader's guides for the teen or youth leader

Need books for your entire crew?

For more information on church and youth group discounts, call: (800) 679-1957
Direct2Church@BakerPublishingGroup.com

 **Revell**
a division of Baker Publishing Group
www.revellbooks.com

 Hungry Planet

www.hungryplanet.net